Plan Your Success

Plan Your Success
Turn Your Dreams into Reality

Gary Slavin

Published by Gary Slavin, Longwood, Florida

© 2009 by Gary Slavin
Printed in the United States of America

ISBN: 978-0-615-31811-0

Library of Congress Control Number: 2009909184

Edited by Arthur H. Slavin

Cover Design by Carolyn Sheltraw
www.csheltraw.com

Format and Layout by Brenda Judy
www.publishersplanet.com

Photos in chapters 1, 3–11 and appendix courtesy of
office.microsoft.com/clipart

This book is printed on acid-free paper.

www.garyslavin.com

Contents

Acknowledgements

My mother and father always supported everything I strived to achieve and gave me the freedom to do what I wanted in my career. I know if they were with us today, they would be so proud that I've finally written this book, something I've always talked about doing and have now accomplished.

This book would not have been possible if not for all the prospects and clients I've worked with in the last twenty years who, prior to our meeting, believed having plans in their heads was all they needed. Refining the process over the years as I assisted so many of them gave me the passion and inspiration to turn this book into reality. I thank them all for making me realize how helpful this book will be for anyone struggling to make it happen.

Thank you to all my friends and colleagues that kept asking when I'd finish and kept pushing me on. A big thank you to my brother, whose expert editorial skills and general content advice definitely made this book better, as well as to Jo Crimmins for her valuable input. On the production side, thanks to Brenda Judy for her advice and formatting skills to make this book look professional. And I can't forget Evan Finer, whose success with his own book drove me to complete a book of my own . . . not that we were in competition!

No matter how many people I thank, I know I've probably forgotten someone. So, if you're reading this page and looking for your name and it's not here, forgive me and know I appreciated your assistance.

Chapter One

Introduction

A Need to Dream

When an artist begins to paint a scene
Or like a movie theatre with an empty screen . . .
Is that how our lives would really seem
If we weren't allowed to dream?

For what is life without some fantasy
Like being lost, alone on a ship at sea?
Living each day with the same routine
If we weren't allowed to dream.

A dream so vivid as to almost be real,
You want to reach out and actually feel
What it is you've wanted year after year . . .
Kept from reaching because of your fear.

The fear of failure we all happen upon
When the crown of logic is what we don.
Satisfaction in merely accomplishing the mean
If we weren't allowed to dream.

Become that artist and paint that scene.
Fill the movie theatre with a life serene.
Reach way out for that elusive beam.
It will happen when you do more than dream!

Yes, we all dream. Young boys and girls dream about becoming accomplished athletes performing in the ultimate competition and succeeding. As adults, we may dream of winning the lottery and obtaining the possessions we've always hoped for. Some dreams are reachable while others are pure whimsy. Dreams of finding the elusive "golden goose'" and living on "easy street" are fantasy. Dreaming about utilizing our talents to accomplish great things is not. Most of us put equal thought into both types, rarely accomplishing either.

We listen to motivational speakers telling us to have goals that will turn our dreams into reality. They tell us to write our goals down and put them on our bathroom mirror or over our computer monitor at work and view them every day. I tried this, and you know what happened? I was able to read my goals every day. That's it! For years, one of my goals was to write a book and have it published. I started two books prior to this one and didn't finish either one. And that wasn't the only goal I had that was never realized.

Just writing the goals down was not making them happen. What was missing was a plan. This missing ingredient is what motivated me to develop a simple four-step process for planning. The objective is to turn dreams into goals, and then break them down into actions that will result in the realization of those dreams.

My method is the result of over twenty years of research, as well as the application of principles of strategic planning and implementation. I will walk you down a proven path to turn your dreams into reality. You will learn how to create personal and business goals and align them, ensuring that both of these important aspects of your life are equally successful. Finally, I will show you how to create action steps that will allow you to accomplish both sets of goals.

A word of warning before you turn the page and begin your journey toward success: The trip you are about to take consists of four simple, easy-to-follow steps. But don't let the word "easy" fool you. The process may be easy to understand, but you must do the work. So, let's get started!

Chapter Two

The Planning Premise

Why Plan?

Being spontaneous can be fun. So why not just have meaningful and measurable goals and go for it? Anyone who has dreamed of and then had a perfect wedding can answer that question. There is so much planning involved to ensure everything turns out perfect. And, just like the wedding, there is planning involved in any event. Construction sites involve complex planning to make certain the bridge, building and road are completed on time, within budget, and that they pass inspection.

The list goes on and on. I wouldn't start this book without an outline and a plan of action. Have you ever taken a driving vacation without first mapping out your route? Have you ever given a presentation without making notes? How about the time you finally bought your dream car? Before going to the dealership you knew how much you could afford, what interest rate you needed to keep your payment at your *planned* amount and the color you wanted. Sounds like a plan to me.

I have a friend in Ohio who owns a boat. What if he drove to his favorite Lake Erie boat launch, backed the boat down the launch and drifted out onto the lake. Where would he wind up? He has a plan every time he takes his boat out. He knows whether he's going fishing, to visit someone on the lake or just out for a ride. He has a separate plan for each goal or he'd wind up letting the currents take him wherever and ultimately get lost.

Students dreaming of becoming doctors and lawyers can't just go through school spontaneously hoping to someday get the proper education. They need to carefully plan their class selection and then execute the plan by taking and passing every class. And what about the professors teaching those classes? Don't they plan each semester, each class, to enable students to learn what is stated in the course catalogue?

These examples illustrate that planning is critical in our personal lives and in business. Maybe you're already aware of the statistic that 85 percent of business start-ups fail in the first five years. Recent Small Business Administration (SBA) figures are a bit more optimistic indicating a failure rate for start-up businesses of 34 percent in the first two years, 50 percent after four years and 60 percent after six years or more (source: www.sba.gov/advo/stats/bh_sbe03.pdf). These are better numbers, but still not something we should be excited about.

My research indicates the reasons for these failures are a lack of funding and poor planning. I contend the major reason for these failures is strictly a lack of planning. If business people planned properly in the first place, they would have a good idea of how much capital is necessary to sustain the business during the growth stages.

Well, the SBA keeps statistics on businesses, but not for individuals. A study conducted by the Harvard Business School between 1979 and 1989 revealed that only 3 percent of those surveyed had written goals and plans. Ten years later, it was learned that the 97 percent who did not have written plans were earning ten times *less* than the other 3 percent. Once again, the reasons for this are a lack of a good plan and poor implementation.

Would you ever go on a vacation without planning it first? You'd want to have enough money for your trip. You'd know if you were going to fly or drive, where you were staying, what you were going to see, etc. You know from experience that you're going to have a lot more fun if you know ahead of time what you're going to be doing, where you're going to do it, if the time is right and if everything is available.

So, if we want to be successful in business and in life, we must plan for our success. With a plan, we know we'll have more fun on vacation, our lives will be richer, less stressful and we'll have more time for the things we want to enjoy. And the plan must be written.

Why written? A plan that exists solely in your head is a headache just waiting to happen. So many times I have asked prospects if they had a business plan. The response I get almost every time is, "Yes, it's in my head." When I ask what happens to the plan when a client or vendor calls at three in the afternoon to cancel a major order, they usually laugh without responding. I then ask them how big their headache is when they attempt to reorganize the plan that's in their head. Again, I receive no response.

Eighty percent of the time, I'll get a call the next day. "Someone did call after I left and cancelled a major order." On the way home, the prospect attempted to redo their plan in his head, resulting in a major headache before dinner. They then ask me, "When can you come in to help document my plan?"

Just having goals won't make them happen. You must focus on how to make them become reality. Developing a plan gives you focus. In the following chapters, we'll see that going through the planning process also validates your goals, emphasizes their importance and highlights what you want to achieve.

Chapter Three

Four Key Elements of Success

Motivation, Commitment, Planning and Implementation

Before starting to use the four-step process to achieve success, one needs to appreciate the benefits of motivation, commitment, planning and implementation. These four elements will assist you in getting started, staying on task and working the process until your dreams become reality. These basic principles are the driving force behind the process; therefore, you must not only be aware of them and use them, but fully understand what they will do for you.

Motivation

If you leave something to chance, it probably won't happen. With only luck on your side, odds are you'll go through life with unrealized dreams. No one can force you to do something—if you want to make things happen, the ability to motivate yourself is crucial.

Interest and desire are two important contributors to motivation, and when combined become key factors in your success. Students who want to learn enjoy school and usually perform better than those students who go to school simply to get a diploma or degree. Students who know what they want to do when they graduate have a purpose and tend to pay more attention to their studies. These students are interested in gathering information and have a desire to learn. They motivate themselves to go to school every day.

CEOs don't work their way up the corporate ladder by depending on just their skills or being lucky. It takes more than ability to make it to the top of most corporations. These individuals love what they are doing, care about the success of their company and have a desire to succeed.

Now that you can appreciate how interest and desire affect your motivation, let's look at *want and need*. Have you ever thought about the difference between wanting something and needing something? People are often more interested in obtaining something they want as opposed to something they need. Purchasing power aside, you know you would definitely be more excited about shopping for a new HDTV than for a new refrigerator. We usually grumble about replacing a refrigerator, but anxiously start checking prices and comparing specifications of big screen sets the moment we watch a favorite movie, sporting event or other program on our friend's 42" HDTV. We soon become extremely motivated to check *Consumer Reports*, the Internet and numerous other sources to determine the best HDTV we can find. We motivate ourselves to get that TV . . . and we can wait for a new refrigerator if the current one isn't broken.

How motivated are you to learn, or even pay attention, in the training class that your manager makes you attend? Are you as interested as you were the time you took that night class on photography or dance? You needed to go to one class for your job, but you wanted to go to the evening class you paid for. Your motivation was definitely higher when you attended the class you chose yourself.

You're definitely going to be more motivated to seek out your "dream job" or start your own business than you would be if you just took a job to make some money. Motivation comes from within and helps you stay on task and make something happen. But you need more than just motivation to ensure that this process will work for you.

Commitment

You need to be passionate about accomplishing your goals, not letting anything stop you. You must work hard to make the goals become a reality and tell yourself **you will** make them happen, **not** *you will try* to make them happen.

There is a major difference between "you will try" and "you will." You must eliminate complacency and strive for continuous improvement.

> *Desire is the key to motivation, but it's determination and commitment to an unrelenting pursuit of your goal—a commitment to excellence—that will enable you to attain the success you seek.*
> ~ Mario Andretti

> *There's a difference between interest and commitment. When you're interested in doing something, you do it only when circumstances permit. When you're committed to something, you accept no excuses, only results.*
> ~ Thinkexist.com

Professional athletes seeking an "All-Star" year leave nothing to chance. The "best of the best" professionals are committed to making every year better than the previous one in order to become an All-Star. This takes hard work and commitment.

> *I have always dreamed and set goals to make it to an event like this, and maybe do it several times in your career [sic]. Coming off last year, where things didn't go as well as I would have liked, I set smaller goals of just wanting to be an everyday position player in the major leagues.*
> ~ Carlos Quentin, 2008 Chicago White Sox, after being voted onto the American League all-star team for the first time.

Planning

Not planning leaves room for failure. You must see the path to the finish line before taking your first step. You need to know what you have to do every step of the way to ensure your goals become reality. Planning helps you organize your activities and becomes your roadmap to success. Chapter Two, "The Planning Premise," explained in detail why planning is a critical element in the four-step process. We'll discuss further how to develop a plan in Chapter Eight, "Create Your Plan for Success."

Implementation

"If you plan it, it will happen," is an oversimplification I use only to make a point about the importance of planning. Even the best researched, well-written plan is just a pile of papers if it's never implemented.

Having a plan makes your outcome possible and reduces the effort needed to achieve your desired result. But just having a plan will not make it happen. **You** still have to make it happen. In Chapter Nine, "Implementing Your Plan for Success," we will discuss the steps that are necessary to turn your plan into reality.

Chapter Four

*The Four Steps to Success:
An Overview*

Four Easy Steps
for Planning Your Success

For some of us, our dreams are what keep us going. But it can be frustrating when all you have are empty unfulfilled dreams:

- I want to be famous someday

- I want to be a well-known author

- I want to change my career

- I want to be a world-class athlete

- I want to become a famous actor

- I want to be a social worker

- I want to be a millionaire

- I want to retire at an early age

Those sound like typical dreams we think about or hear every day. To be happier and more successful, however, we need to turn our dreams into reality. The problem is that our dreams, similar to the ones written above, are often so vague and general that it is nearly impossible for us to focus on making them happen. What we need is a process for dealing with this dilemma.

Here are the four easy steps for planning your success:

1. Turn your dreams into personal goals

2. Create business/job goals

3. Align your personal and business/job goals

4. Create your plan for success

Step 1: Turn Your Dreams into Personal Goals

"The difference between a goal and a dream is the written word."
~ Gene Donohue

Just writing out your dream doesn't make it a goal.

A dream is something we wish will happen, while a goal has a purpose and an anticipated result. A goal must include the actions required for achieving the desired outcome. First, you need to visualize what you want to have, feel and experience in life before writing out your goals. Then use the SMART model to ensure the goals are actionable and specific enough for you to be able to accomplish them.

SMART goals are Specific, Measurable, Attainable, Realistic and Timely.

Specific

Specific goals are clear-cut and point out **what** you want to accomplish, **why** this is important to you, **how** you are going to reach the goal and **who** is involved. Specifics give you more focus and identify key action items. Making your goal specific emphasizes what you want to happen and increases the likelihood that it will be accomplished.

Measurable

Establish criteria for determining how you are progressing toward reaching your goal. If you can't measure it, you will never know if you've accomplished it. Milestones enable you to gauge your progress, stay on track, reach target dates and celebrate minor successes. Reaching each milestone will give you the encouragement to keep working toward reaching the result. Be specific with your milestones by answering questions like "how much" and "how many," so you know exactly when you've accomplished the goal.

"I will lose fifteen pounds over the next six months" is measurable in time and outcome, while "I want to lose some weight" is not.

Attainable

We've all heard the saying, "See the light at the end of the tunnel." You should set goals that will challenge you and give you a sense of accomplishment, but, at the same time, make sure the targets you establish are within your reach. When they are, you develop the attitudes, abilities and skills required to reach them. Set goals you believe you can accomplish. Your goals should be doable!

A well-developed and implemented plan will enable you to realize any goal you set, and with each small victory, gain the confidence to accomplish even more. Your skill level will increase with each triumph, making it possible for you to stretch and reach even greater degrees of success.

Realistic

Keep in mind that you are setting goals to help you reach your next level of success and that you will need to stretch to get there. "Realistic," therefore, should not be mistaken for "easy."

Determine whether the goal represents a next step in your life or a leap into something new. If new, you need to ascertain what skills, if any, you already possess that will facilitate this leap. The goal should represent something you want to and believe you can accomplish, thus giving you the motivational force to grow and succeed in this endeavor.

Timely

When do you expect the goals to become a reality—next week, next month? Set a time frame that will give you a target to work toward and that creates a sense of urgency.

Step 2: Create Business/Job Goals

Business or job goals, unlike personal goals, are not normally derived from dreams, but from what we strive to accomplish at work for the business and ourselves. In this step, you will be describing why you work and exactly what it is you want to achieve through your business or job. You should think about what it is that makes you want to go to work every day. Keep in mind that your reasons may vary based on whether you own your own business or work for someone.

Step 3: Align Your Personal and Business/Job Goals

The third step is to evaluate your personal and business/job goals and make sure they are aligned. Make certain both sets of goals match and can be achieved. If not, you won't accomplish either set of goals, and both your business and personal life will suffer. If necessary, you need to determine how to modify your goals so that your business and personal lives complement each other. You might have to change jobs or make changes to your business in order to reach your personal goals. If your goals aren't aligned and you don't make any adjustments, you will be unhappy at work. This will definitely carry over to your personal life.

Step 4: Create Your Plan for Success

Once you've aligned both sets of goals, you are ready for the fourth and final step: creating your plan for success. This is where you make your job or business work for you. Put a plan in place to ensure that your goals become reality. You do this by developing a set of objectives, strategies and tactics to accomplish each goal. This becomes your blueprint for success.

If you plan it well and follow through on that plan, it will happen. As I mentioned before, a documented plan will eliminate many headaches and enable you to look over your goals, objectives and strategies and, using a pen or pencil, make minor changes that account for any unplanned occurrence. This is much simpler and less painful than trying to reorganize a plan that exists solely in your head.

Success isn't something that will come knocking on your door. Only you can make it happen. You need to turn your dreams into SMART personal and business goals, align your goals and create your plan for success.

We all have a need to dream, but you need to do more than dream to become truly successful.

Chapter Five

Step 1:
Turn Your Dreams
into Personal Goals

Creating SMART Personal Goals

Which of the following is a SMART personal goal?

- I want to change my career.

- I want to be able to golf more.

I hope you answered that neither one is a SMART goal. What are we trying to accomplish? When will it be completed? These and several more questions still need to be resolved to make these SMART goals.

This is how to restate these into SMART goals:

- I will ensure that I have or will develop the skills necessary for the new career I have chosen, update my resume accordingly, and find a new job within six months.

- Within the next three months I am going to change my schedule at home to ensure I have enough free time to be able to golf every Saturday and still spend quality time with my family.

Now you know exactly what needs to be accomplished and by when. There is no room for misinterpretation. You have criteria against which you can measure your progress and determine if and when the goal has been met.

Knowing how to create SMART goals will assist you in creating a goal for each of your dreams. You can use the worksheet in Appendix A or use a separate sheet of paper. Before you do, let's take one of the dreams from the beginning of Chapter Four and walk through how to document your goals.

Let's work with, "I want to become a famous actor."

I chose this one because it really shows how real, yet vague, some dreams can be when you write them down and read them. What is meant by famous? What type of acting do you want to be famous for? When is someday? How will you know when you are considered famous? None of these are addressed in the statement of our dream. Turning this dream into a SMART goal will address this issue.

Now, here's the process:

1. Start with a statement

    a. What do you want to achieve? Be specific!

    b. Make this one simple sentence.

    c. What you're doing at this point is documenting your dream. You're getting it in writing.

2. Next, complete your thought process

    a. Add more detail.

    b. Make this goal SMART.

Seems easy enough, doesn't it? Well, it is. Let's apply this process to our example dream:

1. Before I reach the age of 29, I want to be recognized by the Film Actors Guild as one of their members.

2. When I reach my 29th birthday, I want to have been in at least fifteen top grossing movies, have won an Oscar and be recognizable to at least 80 percent of the U.S. population.

That is a SMART goal. Now turn to Appendix A and create your personal SMART goals. Once you've documented your personal goals, go to Chapter Six and we'll discuss your business SMART goals.

Chapter Six

Step 2:
Create Business/Job Goals

Creating SMART Business/Job Goals

Which of the following is a SMART business/job goal?

- Increase corporate revenue.

- I want to earn a million dollars.

If you read the previous chapter, I know you answered that neither one is a SMART goal. The same questions and criteria apply to these goals as our personal goals. What are we trying to accomplish? When will it be completed? These and several more questions still need to be resolved to make these SMART goals.

This is how to restate these into SMART goals:

- Increase revenue from Government business by 15 percent over the same quarter last year by the second quarter of 2009.

- I want to earn a million dollars selling cosmetics from my home to women between the ages 18 to 65 within the first two years of business.

Now you know exactly what needs to be accomplished and by when. There is no room for misinterpretation. You have criteria against which you can measure your progress and determine if and when the goal has been met.

Now we're ready to focus on creating your own SMART business/job goals.

If you own your own business, you need to consider these questions:

1. What do you want from your business?

    a. Revenue

    b. Image

    c. Leads

    d. Take into account any other purpose or mission that you have for your business.

2. Why did you start your business?

3. Where do you see your business in five years?

If you're working for someone, your goals should address these questions:

1. What do you want from your job?

    a. Money

    b. Success

    c. Recognition

    d. Any other tangibles that you want to take away from your job.

2. Why are you working?

3. Where do you want to be in five years?

These questions are just a starting point. No one knows better than you do about your business or why you are working. Answer these questions to formulate your goals and remember to make them SMART goals.

Turn to Appendix A and, under the business section, write out your business/job goals. Remember to use the same two-step process you employed for documenting your personal goals. Start with simple statements and then complete your thought process by adding more detail. Make your goals Specific, Measurable, Attainable, Realistic and Timely. Go on to Chapter Seven once you've documented your goals.

Chapter Seven

Step 3:
Align Your Personal and
Business/Job Goals

Aligning Your Goals

This is a critical, but often neglected, step in planning your success.

You've documented your personal and business/job goals and now you need to make sure they are aligned. You need to make certain that both sets of goals match and can be achieved. Unless you unify your goals there will be goal conflict, which will foster turmoil in your life and affect your performance on the job. You may not accomplish either set of goals, and both your business and personal life will more than likely suffer.

If you are comfortable that both sets of goals are achievable and, after careful consideration, you determine there are no conflicts, you are ready to move on to Step 4 and start creating your plan for success. However, if this isn't the case, you need to determine how to modify your goals so that your business and personal lives complement each other.

You might have to change jobs, turn down an attractive promotion or make changes to your business in order to reach your personal goals. You might have to reconsider buying that expensive boat or new set of golf clubs if the purchase will cause you to veer off plan. If your goals aren't aligned and you don't make any adjustments, you will be unhappy at work. This will definitely carry over to your personal life.

For the best results, you need to be at ease with the fact that both sets of goals make sense and will ensure that you fulfill all of your personal and professional dreams. For the sake of discussion, let's assume you want to have a fulfilling family life and still want to have a rewarding and successful career. You're in dental school and close to graduation. As you start planning for your professional career, you realize the time commitment involved in setting up and running a dental practice may interfere with your family life. Now is the time to align your goals. You need to determine what can be done to ensure your professional career doesn't interfere with your family life. Check out your options and make the proper adjustments. Maybe you can find a business partner, work for an association, the Veterans Administration or find some way to minimize the time needed to run a private practice.

This example may not fit your situation, but you get the point. If, for you, there is more to life than a career, and at the end of your successful career, all you have is a large net worth, a family of strangers and a list of unfulfilled dreams, you didn't align your personal and business goals effectively.

Keep in mind that there might very well be trade-offs in the process of aligning your goals. You must weigh your options and make the choices that support a healthy and happy life for you as well as the other important people you care about.

Chapter Eight

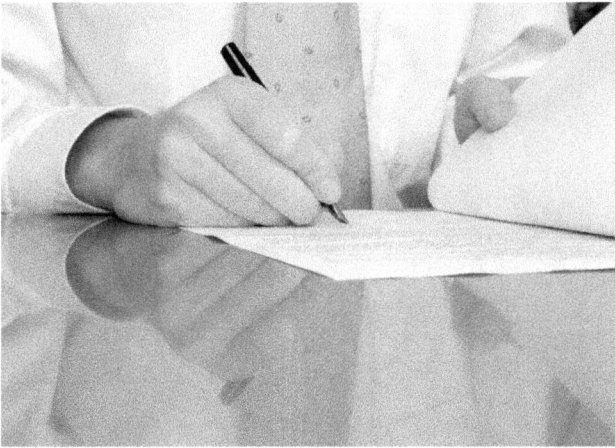

Step 4:
Create Your
Plan for Success

A Simple Planning Process

The planning process I've developed and that you are about to learn is very simple. But don't be fooled by its simplicity. Completing this process is going to take time and thought. I will clarify the process for you in order to maximize the effect of your effort to accomplish your goals.

Even though there is an entire chapter in this book (Chapter Two, "The Planning Premise") devoted to the benefits of planning and documenting your plan, I want to emphasize this again since I've encountered so many people that still believe having a plan in their head is all that is necessary.

1. Going through the process of writing down your plan helps you to crystallize your ideas and refine your plan, thus increasing the chances of your success. Dwight Eisenhower said, "Plans are useless but planning is indispensable."

2. Having the plan documented simplifies making any necessary changes in midstream.

3. Having the plan in black and white is essential for the creation of a "war board." A "war board," which is covered in the next chapter, "Implementing Your Plan for Success," when used properly, will greatly enhance your ability to execute your plan.

Unlike some marketing and business plans that are unnecessarily elaborate, prose laden and go mostly unread, your plans for success will be outlines that are simple to follow. You will develop a separate outline for your personal plan and one for your business/job plan. Each outline will consist of four sections. The sections are:

1. Goals

2. Objectives

3. Strategies

4. Tactics

So far it looks simple, doesn't it? Well, it is. But how many times have you had something explained and then encountered all types of issues when you started to use a so-called simple process? Let's define our terms and then walk through some examples to make sure this doesn't happen to you.

Goals

At this point, you should have a very good idea of how SMART goals are defined within this process. If you still have questions about SMART goals, please review Chapters Five and Six.

Objectives

Goals and objectives are sometimes viewed as interchangeable, even more so when dealing with SMART goals. However, in this process there are differences between the two. Your SMART goals, even though specific and measurable, can tend to be broad, making them difficult, if not impossible, to achieve. This can frustrate your efforts to turn them into reality.

I recommend breaking your goals down into two or more objectives. Each objective should have a singular focus explaining what needs to be accomplished in order to satisfy that portion of

46

the goal it represents. Not to complicate matters, but this is one area where I do leave the final decision up to you. If you feel your goals are succinct enough and developing objectives is more redundant than helpful, you can skip this section.

Strategies

A strategy explains *how* you propose to achieve an objective or goal. Each strategy represents a scheme or action designed to meet the criteria set in the associated objective. You may find it necessary to develop multiple strategies in order to accomplish an objective.

Tactics

You may already be familiar with tactics and their purpose, having seen them referred to as programs, actions or tasks. Tasks are the activities required to accomplish a strategy. Tactics, as defined here, are a bit more specific. They state exactly what needs to be done to achieve an associated strategy. They should include a budget, a time line, and the person or persons responsible to ensure the tasks are completed.

To summarize, using this planning process assists you in breaking down your dream-inspired SMART goals into clear-cut objectives. Next, you create the strategies to meet your objectives and finally develop the tactics that will fulfill the strategies. You will have produced a set of activities which, when completed, will have turned your dreams into reality. The tactics become your roadmap to success.

Now is a good time to walk through some examples just in case you're still scratching you head, wondering how to get started and where to go from here. Once you see how it's done, you'll be able to develop your own plans for success.

Seeing how to break down personal and business/job goals into their component parts will give you a solid understanding of how this process works. After reading through the following examples, you will have the confidence you need to begin creating your own plans.

EXAMPLE ONE: Personal

Dream: I want to be a better golfer.

Goal: I want to reduce my handicap from a 25 Index to an 18 Index in one year or less while playing competitively only once a week.

Note: This is a simple, yet SMART goal. It states what is specifically wanted, how to measure if it's been accomplished, reaching an 18 handicap, and is attainable and realistic with a definitive time frame.

Objectives:

1. Determine my current handicap before the first week of January 2010 and re-evaluate it in December.

2. Determine and utilize the best method for improving my golf game by the second week of January 2010.

3. Determine the least expensive means for playing every week in 2010.

Note: As we stated earlier, goals and objectives are similar, but in this case, the objectives break down the goal into more focused and actionable items.

Now we need to develop the strategies for each objective, designed to ensure it is accomplished.

Let's work with Objective 2: *Determine and utilize the best method for improving my golf game by the second week of January 2010.*

Strategies:

1. Find the best golf professional I can afford on a regular basis.

2. Practice between weekly golf rounds to reinforce the lessons.

3. Find a group in my area that plays every Saturday.

Tactics:

1. Sign up for lessons with a golf professional on January 20.

2. Start taking weekly lessons January 21 and then every Wednesday for five weeks.

3. Go to the driving range every Friday after work.

4. Contact and join a Saturday group in my area and start playing on January 24.

These tactics will ensure the criteria of the strategies are met. The strategies were developed to accomplish this objective. Achieving the objective makes certain that the goal and, thus, the dream is realized! Once you put in the work to develop the plan, realizing your dream becomes that much easier.

Now let's work through a business example using one of the dreams listed at the beginning of Chapter Four.

EXAMPLE 2: Business

Dream: I want to be a well-known author.

Goal: I want to have a book published on strategic planning that will reach the top 250 in sales on Amazon.com, enabling me to increase public speaking engagements and my name recognition by the second quarter of 2010.

Note: Once again, we have what reads as a simple, yet SMART goal. However, there is more that must be accomplished to reach this goal, making planning essential. This type of goal illustrates the need for objectives.

Objectives:

1. Complete the book, *Plan Your Success: Turn Your Dreams Into Reality*, by the third quarter of 2009.

2. Determine and select the best publishing method by the third quarter of 2009.

3. Obtain an agreement with Amazon.com and at least two other distributors by the fourth quarter of 2009.

4. Track and measure book sales starting in the first quarter of 2010.

5. Track and measure the increase in speaking engagements for 2010 over 2009.

Note: In this instance the objectives break down the goal into even more focused areas enabling one to develop specific strategies to ensure the objectives and goal are accomplished.

Let's continue by creating strategies for Objective 2: *Determine and select the best publishing method by the third quarter of 2009.*

Strategies:

1. Interview authors I know to find out how they published their books.

2. Use the Internet to learn as much as possible about publishing in today's market.

3. Use the Internet to learn about publishing using traditional publishers and self-publishing companies.

4. Find out how the majority of books are published today.

Tactics:

1. Each day during the second quarter of 2009, call, e-mail, or use a social networking site to contact at least one friend who has authored a book to find out how they published their book.

2. Create a pro-and-con list to evaluate whether to use traditional or self-publishing.

3. Select a publishing method and, if necessary, contact a publishing company.

4. Have the book published and ready for distribution.

Let's try one more example, this time addressing a job goal.

EXAMPLE 3: Job

Goal: Obtain corporate revenues of $4.5 million by the end of 2009.

Objectives:

1. Obtain 15 percent of total revenue from Government sector new product sales starting in the second quarter of 2009.

2. Obtain 45 percent of total revenue from Private sector new product sales by year-end 2009.

3. Obtain 40 percent of total revenue from service and maintenance contracts by year-end 2009.

Let's develop strategies for Objective 3: *Obtain 40 percent of total revenue from service and maintenance contracts by year-end 2009.*

Strategies:

1. Survey existing customers to determine which elements of the service and maintenance programs are the most beneficial.

2. Create new advertising campaigns for service and maintenance programs and have them placed no later than second quarter of 2009.

3. Get sales staff to increase focus on selling service and maintenance programs.

4. Create sales tools to assist the sales force in selling service and maintenance programs.

Tactics:

1.   Create survey questionnaire.

2.   Conduct phone survey of existing customers.

3.   Develop new advertisements during quarter one.

4.   Select proper media for advertisements.

5.   Contact publications and place advertisements starting in quarter two.

6.   Create new compensation incentives for 2009 to guide the sales force to focus on increasing service and maintenance program sales.

7.   Create new sales slicks to match new ads.

Note: The tactics above were written as single sentences for readability and are sufficient for demonstrating the process. However, each of your business/job tactics should include a budget, time line and an individual responsible for completing the task.

You may have noticed similarities as you read the above examples, detecting some trends in the resulting objectives, strategies and tactics. These trends will make it easier for you to duplicate the process. The more you follow and use this process, the easier it will become for you to develop comprehensive plans that, when followed, will ensure you reach your goals.

Turn to Appendix B and, using the personal and business/job goals you created in Appendix A; complete your plans by developing the objectives, strategies and tactics necessary to realize your goals.

Go on to the next chapter once you've documented your plans.

Chapter Nine

*Implementing Your
Plan for Success*

Your Plans are Written . . . Now What?

It's time to implement your plan. Technically, implementation is not an actual step in the planning process, but without it, all your hard work will have been for nothing. Much has been written about strategic planning but not much about implementing the plan. I find it fascinating that as necessary as plan execution is, it is so often neglected. One of the most important jobs that strategic planning, marketing and business consultants have is ensuring that their clients follow through on the strategies and tactics they have developed together. Now that your plans are written, implementation must be your major focus.

Why is it that after devoting so much time and effort to planning, few people or organizations take the next step and carry out the tactics? Could it be that the thought of completing all the tactics makes one's head spin and causes them to freeze trying to figure out where to start? If that's the case, and I'm confident it is most of the time, then we need some way to simplify implementing a well-structured plan. This is why I came up with the war board.

What is a war board? You can call it your activity chart, implementation planner . . . whatever works for you. I first started calling it a war board when I was the marketing director for a training organization that was competing with two other companies for market share. We developed a strategic plan to take over the lead and win the "war" for market share. I used an erasable white board in my office to list all the tactics from our plan. Now I had all the daily tasks for every marketing team member in one easily accessible and visible place.

The board also served to show everyone on the team where we were, relative to accomplishing our goals. We met every morning for fifteen minutes to determine what was recently completed, what we missed and what we needed to address that day.

It may not be necessary for you to review the chart every day, or list out tasks every day, but you do need to decide on a frequency and stick to it. Regardless of your time frame, the reviews must be on a regular basis to enable you to make any necessary modifications to dates, budgets, et cetera to ensure you stay on plan. There may even be times when, based on your review, you have to go back and modify a strategy, objective or goal.

This method is similar to using a "to be done today" list. The major difference with the war board is that all the tasks are taken from your personal or business plan. The tasks tie back to the strategies created to accomplish the objectives derived from your goals. You are using this chart to keep moving forward and to assist in tracking your progress toward turning your dreams into reality.

The chart is a very simple matrix. You place your timetable across the top, team members or individuals responsible for task completion along the left side, and the associated tasks in each cell. The war board could look something like the one on the following page if we were to use the tactics for Objective 3 (Obtain 40 percent of total revenue from service and maintenance contracts by year-end 2009) from our job example in the previous chapter.

Having this chart, or one similar to it, causes you to focus on each task without the anxiety triggered by thinking about all the tasks required to accomplish your entire plan. As each task is completed, you can either remove it from the chart or place a check mark in the corresponding cell.

Business Strategy Progress

Task Owner	January	February	March	April	May	June
Bill W			Write survey questions	Place new ads		
Anne T		Develop new ads	Create new sales literature			
Anne T			Select ad media			
Tina B				Start phone survey	Cont. phone survey	Complete survey by end of month
Boss	Create sales comp incentives					

The chart also assists you in tracking your progress. Come February if there isn't a check mark next to "create sales comp incentives," you know you're behind schedule on this task and are possibly jeopardizing completing this objective on time. In any case, it enables you to track your progress toward your goals and make any necessary changes to dates, budgets, et cetera, if required.

Having a chart enables you and your team members (if applicable) to focus on individual tasks on a regular basis. This will ensure you continue to implement your plan to completion.

Chapter Ten

What to do . . . If

Your Recovery Plan

Task Owner	January	February	March	April	May	June
Business Strategy Progress						
Bill W			Write survey questions	Place new ads		
Anne T		**Develop new ads**	Create new sales literature			
Anne T			Select ad media			
Tina B				Start phone survey	Cont. phone survey	Complete survey by end of month
Boss	**Create sales comp incentives**					

It's the beginning of March and the two underlined tasks have yet to be completed. What can be done? How do we recover? These are two excellent questions, and they emphasize the importance of having a war board or some means of keeping track of your progress toward implementing your plan. You try to avoid situations like this, but we all know what happens when daily "emergencies" arise, or we get busy with other work.

So, what do we do from a planning standpoint when we fall behind on certain tasks? All too often, in team situations, we jump to call a meeting. However, there are better ways to handle this. One possible solution is to meet one-on-one with the individual responsible for the late activity to determine the status and the reasons for missing the date. Once you have all the facts you can and should set a new completion date.

Next, you need to evaluate if and how the changes have affected the associated strategy, objective and goal. Then make any necessary modifications. These modifications can include changing the objective date, the overall budget or even adjustments to other strategies or objectives.

Once that is complete, you need to review the entire plan and determine if there is any global impact. Finally, you need to update the war board and, as you do, check to ascertain if any other tasks need to be changed as a result of moving the dates for this task. For example, you need to determine if this person is still available for other tasks, etc.

You also need to go through this process for your personal plan. You may not have the same people issues, but you'll need to figure out, document and make all the necessary changes to your plan just as you did for the business plan cited above.

Your plans, whether business or personal, must be flexible. You need to review them on a regular basis to assess your progress and take whatever action is necessary to ensure you meet your goals. Having a chart, war board, task list, whatever works for you, will definitely assist in keeping you on track.

Chapter Eleven

*Avoiding the
Planning Pitfalls*

Know What to Avoid

A lot has been written about strategic planning, planning pitfalls and what to avoid during the planning process. But most of it is geared toward corporate planning rather than for turning your individual dreams into reality. This chapter is about what to avoid during the planning and implementation processes for both business and personal plans.

There is some truth to the saying, "if you plan it, it will happen," but you shouldn't take it literally. The phrase is more appropriate if stated this way: "If you don't plan it, it won't happen, unless you're really lucky or all the stars are aligned perfectly for you."

One way to avoid the mistakes frequently encountered during planning and implementation is to follow the procedures and processes in this book. The objective of your plan is to provide you with a guide for achieving your goals and realizing your dreams. **The Four Steps to Success** was developed as a blueprint for planning and implementation as well as how best to evaluate your progress and keep you on track. By carefully adhering to each step, and remembering the four key elements from Chapter Three, "Motivation, Commitment, Planning and Implementation," you will successfully turn your dreams into reality.

You recall we also mentioned in Chapter Three that not planning leaves room for failure. Developing a sound plan makes implementation more straightforward and enables you to avoid many of the implementation missteps. The biggest pitfall is procrastination. Again, motivation and commitment are the keys to avoiding this problem. Creating realistic SMART goals and focused tactics will assist in keeping you motivated and committed to completing your plan.

Another oversight I see often is the failure to execute strategies. What is often missing is an accountability system or an individual responsible for the tasks. This is easily avoided using your war board.

Other pitfalls to avoid include:

- Developing an overwhelming plan

  o Keep your goals SMART to avoid this. Also, don't create more goals than you can realistically accomplish.

- Creating a plan that doesn't correspond to your dreams

  o Developing SMART goals will also avoid this situation.

- Not incorporating implementation into the plan

  o Developing easy-to-follow and understandable tactics will assist in avoiding this one.

  o Setting up and using a war board forces you to implement properly.

- Getting caught up in day-to-day activities

  o Checking and using your war board will definitely help here.

- Neglecting to track your progress

  o Having SMART goals, measurable objectives and time lines for your tactics will keep you on track.

- No accountability

  o Don't just assign someone to a task; hold them accountable even if it's you!

Chapter Twelve

The Finish Line

Congratulations!

At this point you should have your personal and business goals aligned. Both plans should be completed. And two sets of tasks that, when completed, will have you on the doorstep to your dream.

We all have the need to dream, but we need to do more to ensure we enjoy our work and our daily lives. Now you have taken a major step in that direction.

Accomplishing a goal should be fun. If you're not enjoying making it happen, there is something wrong with the goal. Rethink it, making certain that it is one that combines enjoyment with self-improvement and personal growth.

While we're on the subject of rethinking, keep in mind that neither plan should be set in concrete. While in the implementation phase, you should continuously review your goals, objectives and strategies to ensure they are still on target with what you want to accomplish on the job and with your life. If necessary, make adjustments. And if you make any adjustments, make sure both plans are still aligned. If you make a change to a business goal, determine whether the change will impact your personal plan and vice versa. Remember, not aligning your goals can prevent you from achieving your success in addition to making you unhappy at work and in your personal life.

Have fun developing and implementing your plans and you'll start enjoying work more than ever. And to top it all off, your life will be more fulfilled.

If you have questions about the procedures in this book or have any issues regarding the completion of your plans, visit www.garyslavin.com. I'll answer your questions, review your plan or assist you in getting to the next step.

Good luck in your quest to turn your dreams into reality.

Appendices

APPENDIX A:
Let's Get SMART

Remember the process:

1. Start with a statement

    a. What do you want to achieve? Be specific!

    b. Make this one simple sentence.

    c. What you're doing at this point is documenting your dream. You're getting it in writing.

2. Next, complete your thought process

    a. Add more detail.

    b. Make this goal SMART.

Use this process for your personal and business goals. Write a goal statement for each dream on the following worksheets and then complete the process by ensuring that they are specific, measurable, attainable, realistic and timely. If you need more worksheets, simply copy one of the pages in this appendix as many times as necessary.

The SMART goals you develop here will be used for creating your personal and business plans. Remember, documenting these goals now will make the planning process that much easier.

Personal SMART Goals

Goal Statement: _____

_____

_____

SMART Goal 1: _____

_____

_____

SMART Goal Test:

☐ What makes this goal specific? _____

☐ What makes this goal measurable? _____

☐ What makes this goal attainable? _____

☐ What makes this goal realistic? _____

☐ What makes this goal timely? _____

Personal SMART Goals

Goal Statement: _____

_____

_____

SMART Goal 2: _____

_____

_____

SMART Goal Test:

☐ What makes this goal specific? _____

☐ What makes this goal measurable? _____

☐ What makes this goal attainable? _____

☐ What makes this goal realistic? _____

☐ What makes this goal timely? _____

Personal SMART Goals

Goal Statement: _____

_____

_____

SMART Goal 3: _____

_____

_____

SMART Goal Test:

☐ What makes this goal specific? _____

☐ What makes this goal measurable? _____

☐ What makes this goal attainable? _____

☐ What makes this goal realistic? _____

☐ What makes this goal timely? _____

Business SMART Goals

Goal Statement: _____

_____

_____

SMART Goal 1: _____

_____

_____

SMART Goal Test:

☐ What makes this goal specific? _____

☐ What makes this goal measurable? _____

☐ What makes this goal attainable? _____

☐ What makes this goal realistic? _____

☐ What makes this goal timely? _____

Business SMART Goals

Goal Statement: _____

_____

_____

SMART Goal 2: _____

_____

_____

SMART Goal Test:

☐ What makes this goal specific? _____

☐ What makes this goal measurable? _____

☐ What makes this goal attainable? _____

☐ What makes this goal realistic? _____

☐ What makes this goal timely? _____

Business SMART Goals

Goal Statement: _____

_____

_____

SMART Goal 3: _____

_____

_____

SMART Goal Test:

☐ What makes this goal specific? _____

☐ What makes this goal measurable? _____

☐ What makes this goal attainable? _____

☐ What makes this goal realistic? _____

☐ What makes this goal timely? _____

APPENDIX B:
Let The Planning Begin!

Use the following worksheets to expand the goals you developed in Appendix A into your personal and business plans. Remember, if you feel your goals are succinct enough and developing objectives is more redundant than helpful, you can consider going directly from your goals to strategies.

The worksheets are set up so you can work on each goal until you've come up with tactics that, when completed, will ensure you realize your goal. The final step will be to transfer all the tactics to a war board, to-do list or whatever format you prefer.

The format used here is a recommendation. You're welcome to use any format that works best for you. Let me emphasize that getting your plans in writing is far more important than which format you choose. So, let the planning begin!

Personal Plan Worksheet

Goal 1: _____

_____

_____

Objectives:

1. _____

_____

_____

2. _____

_____

_____

3. _____

_____

_____

4. _____

_____

_____

Personal Goal 1 Strategies:

1. _____

_____

_____

_____

2. _____

_____

_____

_____

3. _____

_____

_____

_____

4. _____

_____

_____

_____

Personal Goal 1 Tactics:

1. ____

2. ____

3. ____

4. ____

Personal Goal 2:

_____

_____

_____

Objectives:

1. _____

_____

_____

2. _____

_____

_____

3. _____

_____

_____

4. _____

_____

_____

Personal Goal 2 Strategies:

1. _____

_____

_____

2. _____

_____

_____

3. _____

_____

_____

4. _____

_____

_____

Personal Goal 2 Tactics:

1. _____

_____

_____

_____

2. _____

_____

_____

_____

3. _____

_____

_____

_____

4. _____

_____

_____

_____

Personal Goal 3:

_____

_____

_____

Objectives:

1. _____

_____

_____

2. _____

_____

_____

3. _____

_____

_____

4. _____

_____

_____

Personal Goal 3 Strategies:

1. _____

_____

_____

_____

2. _____

_____

_____

_____

3. _____

_____

_____

_____

4. _____

_____

_____

_____

Personal Goal 3 Tactics:

1. _____

_____

_____

_____

2. _____

_____

_____

_____

3. _____

_____

_____

_____

4. _____

_____

_____

_____

Business Plan Worksheet

Goal 1: _____

_____

_____

Objectives:

1. _____

_____

_____

2. _____

_____

_____

3. _____

_____

_____

4. _____

_____

_____

Business Goal 1 Strategies:

1. _____

_____

_____

_____

2. _____

_____

_____

_____

3. _____

_____

_____

_____

4. _____

_____

_____

_____

Business Goal 1 Tactics:

1. _____

_____

_____

_____

2. _____

_____

_____

_____

3. _____

_____

_____

_____

4. _____

_____

_____

_____

Business Goal 2:

_____

_____

_____

Objectives:

1. _____

_____

_____

2. _____

_____

_____

3. _____

_____

_____

4. _____

_____

_____

Business Goal 2 Strategies:

1. _____

_____

_____

_____

2. _____

_____

_____

_____

3. _____

_____

_____

_____

4. _____

_____

_____

_____

Business Goal 2 Tactics:

1. _____

_____

_____

_____

2. _____

_____

_____

_____

3. _____

_____

_____

_____

4. _____

_____

_____

_____

Business Goal 3:

_____

_____

_____

Objectives:

1. _____

_____

_____

2. _____

_____

_____

3. _____

_____

_____

4. _____

_____

_____

Business Goal 3 Strategies:

1. _____

_____

_____

_____

2. _____

_____

_____

_____

3. _____

_____

_____

_____

4. _____

_____

_____

_____

Business Goal 3 Tactics:

1. _____

_____

_____

_____

2. _____

_____

_____

_____

3. _____

_____

_____

_____

4. _____

_____

_____

_____

About
The Author

Gary Slavin has been working with successful organizations as an independent consultant since 1986, assisting them in determining the best methods for taking their companies to the next level, launching new products and services, or finding unique ways to put life back into and maximize profits for existing product lines. He works with management in developing and implementing business plans, marketing and sales strategies, and then conducts training seminars to ensure that staff members in all departments have the necessary skills to accomplish corporate goals.

Gary has presented seminars to all types of professionals at varying skill levels. Participants attending these seminars have called him a training powerhouse who exhibits endless energy and enthusiasm. His understanding and love of the subject matter enables him to deliver the best training seminars in the business.

He has always been able to motivate participants as well as impart knowledge, enabling them to improve their on-the-job skills and income-generating ability. His approach is down-to-earth for both beginners as well as experienced professionals. In addition, Gary has presented informational seminars on the future of training, marketing, sales, strategic planning and general business strategy. He is always available to speak at conferences, sales meetings or other corporate events.

www.garyslavin.com

www.ingramcontent.com/pod-product-compliance
Lightning Source LLC
LaVergne TN
LVHW021524080426
835509LV00018B/2642